RESPONSIBLE CITIZENSHIP

Jury Duty

by Kirsten Chang

BLASTOFF! READERS

BELLWETHER MEDIA • MINNEAPOLIS, MN

Blastoff! Readers are carefully developed by literacy experts to build reading stamina and move students toward fluency by combining standards-based content with developmentally appropriate text.

Level 1 provides the most support through repetition of high-frequency words, light text, predictable sentence patterns, and strong visual support.

Level 2 offers early readers a bit more challenge through varied sentences, increased text load, and text-supportive special features.

Level 3 advances early-fluent readers toward fluency through increased text load, less reliance on photos, advancing concepts, longer sentences, and more complex special features.

★ **Blastoff! Universe**

Reading Level

Grade **K**

Grades **1–3**

Grade **4**

This edition first published in 2022 by Bellwether Media, Inc.

No part of this publication may be reproduced in whole or in part without written permission of the publisher. For information regarding permission, write to Bellwether Media, Inc., Attention: Permissions Department, 6012 Blue Circle Drive, Minnetonka, MN 55343.

Library of Congress Cataloging-in-Publication Data

Names: Chang, Kirsten, 1991- author.
Title: Jury duty / by Kirsten Chang.
Description: Minneapolis, MN : Bellwether Media, Inc., 2022. | Series: Blastoff! Readers: responsible citizenship | Includes bibliographical references and index. | Audience: Ages 5-8 | Audience: Grades K-1 | Summary: "Developed by literacy experts for students in kindergarten through grade three, this book introduces jury duty to young readers through leveled text and related photos"–Provided by publisher.
Identifiers: LCCN 2021016556 (print) | LCCN 2021016557 (ebook) | ISBN 9781644874974 (library binding) | ISBN 9781648344732 (paperback) | ISBN 9781648344053 (ebook)
Subjects: LCSH: Jury–United States–Juvenile literature.
Classification: LCC KF8972 .C53 2022 (print) | LCC KF8972 (ebook) | DDC 347.73/752–dc23
LC record available at https://lccn.loc.gov/2021016556
LC ebook record available at https://lccn.loc.gov/2021016557

Text copyright © 2022 by Bellwether Media, Inc. BLASTOFF! READERS and associated logos are trademarks and/or registered trademarks of Bellwether Media, Inc.

Editor: Kieran Downs   Designer: Brittany McIntosh

Printed in the United States of America, North Mankato, MN.

Table of Contents

A Fair Trial

Liam is on a jury.
He listens to the **trial**.
He helps choose
what happens.

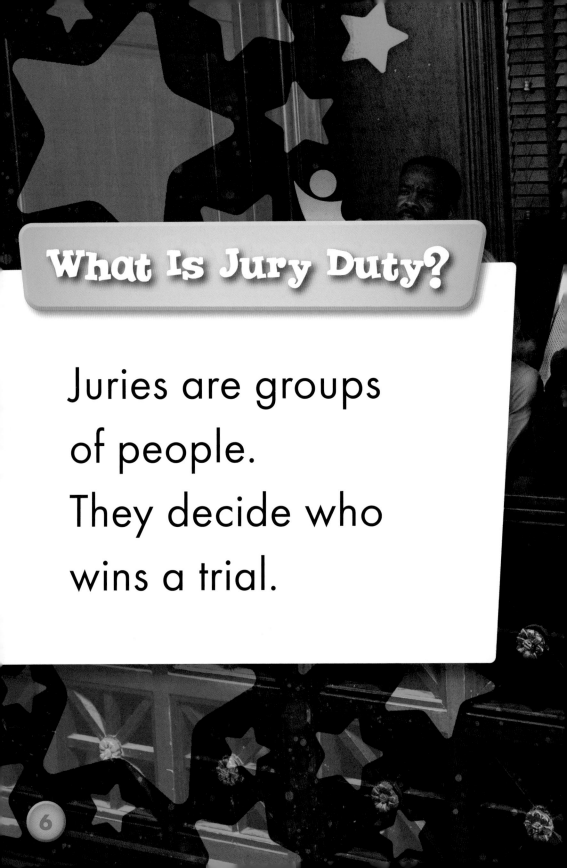

What Is Jury Duty?

Juries are groups of people. They decide who wins a trial.

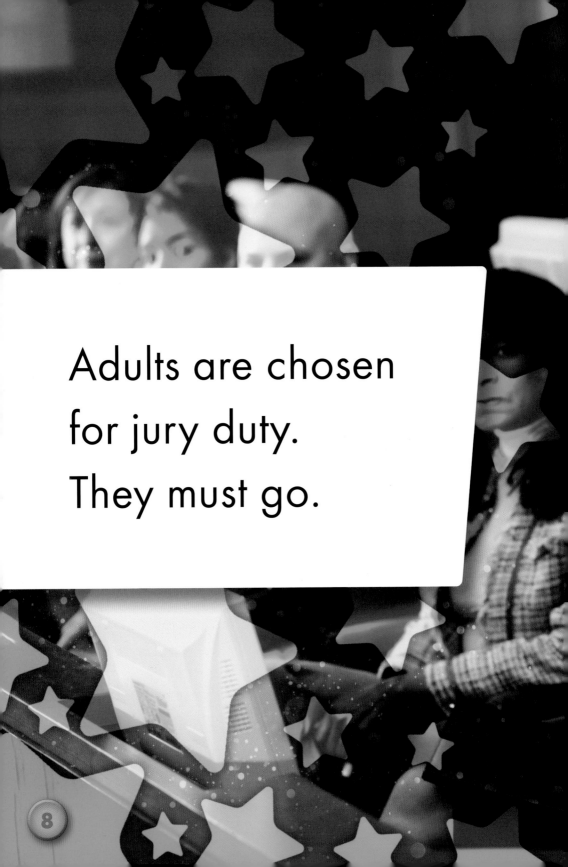

Adults are chosen
for jury duty.
They must go.

Must Haves

- ✓ **United States citizen**
- ✓ **18 years old or older**
- ✓ **speaks English**

Trials are held
in **courts**.
A judge is in charge.

judge

Juries listen to trials.
They hear what
both sides say.

Juries talk about what they heard. They must **agree** on their choice.

Why Is Jury Duty Important?

Juries keep trials fair. Fair trials keep our **rights** safe.

Fair trials also help end **arguments** peacefully.

With/Without

arguments are peaceful

arguments may not be peaceful

Jury duty is an important **task**!

JURORS

Glossary

agree

to have the same beliefs or feelings

rights

powers people have that should not be taken away

arguments

times when people do not agree and fight with words

task

something that has to be done

courts

places where trials take place

trial

an event in which a judge and jury use the law to make a decision

To Learn More

AT THE LIBRARY

Alexander, Vincent. *Serving on a Jury*. Minneapolis, Minn.: Jump!, 2019.

Downs, Kieran. *Judges*. Minneapolis, Minn.: Bellwether Media, 2021.

Rustad, Martha E. H. *Serving on a Jury*. North Mankato, Minn.: Capstone Press, 2020.

ON THE WEB

FACTSURFER

Factsurfer.com gives you a safe, fun way to find more information.

1. Go to www.factsurfer.com.

2. Enter "jury duty" into the search box and click 🔍.

3. Select your book cover to see a list of related content.

Index

The images in this book are reproduced through the courtesy of: sirtravelalot, front cover, pp. 20-21; Alina555, pp. 4-5, 18-19; IPGGutenbergUKLtd, pp. 6-7; dcdebs, pp. 8-9; wavebreakmedia, pp. 10-11; RichLegg, pp. 12-13, 19 (left); Jeff Gilbert/ Alamy Stock Photo, pp. 14-15; Image Source, pp. 16-17; Roman Kosolapov, p. 19 (right); Atstock Productions, p. 22 (agree); Antonio Guillem, p. 22 (arguments); vesperstock, p. 22 (courts); Nirat.pix, p. 22 (rights); Drazen Zigic, p. 22 (task); MR.Yanukit, p. 22 (trial).